# OATMEAL AND A CIGARETTE

*George Sapio*

I0139918

**BROADWAY PLAY PUBLISHING INC**
224 E 62nd St, NY, NY 10065
www.broadwayplaypub.com
info@broadwayplaypub.com

OATMEAL AND A CIGARETTE
© Copyright 2017 George Sapio

Cover art by Billy

First edition: October 2017
I S B N: 978-0-88145-741-4

Book design: Marie Donovan
Page make-up: Adobe InDesign
Typeface: Palatino

OATMEAL AND A CIGARETTE was first produced at the Kitchen Theatre Company in Ithaca, NY, in March 2008. The cast and creative contributor were:

BILLY ............................................................ Daniel J Kiely
CLAIRE ........................................................ Karl Gregory
JANE ............................... Madeline McDonough Maher
*Director* ..................................... Melissa Thompson

OATMEAL AND A CIGARETTE was subsequently produced at the 2008 Cincinnati Fringe Festival and the 2008 New York International Fringe Festival (produced by Bad Dog! Productions) with the same cast and creative contributor.

# ACKNOWLEDGMENTS

Theatre is collaborative. That's one of its joys: the creative interactions that happen among talented and dedicated artists in an effort to make a production the best it can be. OATMEAL AND A CIGARETTE was sparked by a pair of extremely exuberant late-night phone calls to me by actors Karl Gregory and Daniel J Kiely.

I had worked with Dan before several times as a director to his actor, and knew Karl from his many excellent performances at Ithaca, New York's Kitchen Theatre. Each exhorted me to write a play in which they could act together. As it was rather late (or early if you look at things morning-wise) I grumpily hung up on both of them.

They were persistent, however, and one thing led to another, which culminated in the play you now hold in your hands. Along the way we brought in Madeline McDonough Maher to round out the cast, and I asked Melissa Thompson to direct.

The chemistry was perfect. We began with improvisations, and soon we had a basis for the play: a family, but one rather atypical. Further improvisations and discussions ensued, and OATMEAL AND A CIGARETTE began to take form.

I usually write in a vacuum. It was a new experience to write/develop a play with input from actors.

Dan, Karl, Madeline, and Melissa were completely dedicated to Billy, Claire, and Jane. I was challenged by the team's input and obsessively inspired; the writing proved difficult at times but ultimately so very rewarding.

And there are others who need to be recognized. I am grateful to the Kitchen Theatre for providing a space to rehearse, develop, and stage the play for two nights before I took it on the road. The Cincinnati Fringe Festival, which made us feel like we were family, is a place where artistic magic flourishes. And endless thanks to my wife, Maura Stephens, for her unwavering belief in my work and especially this play. I truly cherish her wisdom and insight.

# CHARACTERS & SETTING

CLAIRE, *male, 40s. Highly protective of* BILLY. *Knits a lot.*

BILLY, *male, 30. Bearded. Curious and frustrated. (Note: he is not to be played as a "special" character; he is not mentally impaired in any way.)*

JANE, *female, 20s. Ambitious, determined. Genuinely cares for* BILLY. *Wears glasses.*

*Living room of* CLAIRE *and* BILLY'*s apartment. Many hand-knitted blankets and afghans.*

*Slashes indicate where next actor(s) should overspeak/jump in.*

*The song that opens the play is sung to the tune of* Hush, Little Baby, *a traditional lullaby.*

## Scene I

(CLAIRE *enters from kitchen with a bowl of oatmeal. He crosses to* BILLY*'s crib and sings softly*)

CLAIRE: Mockingbird, little mockingbird
Gonna buy my baby boy a mockingbird
And if that mockingbird tries to fly
Gonna sit on him and make him cry
If he don't cry and tries to sing
Gonna tie him up in my apron string
And if that apron string don't hold
He's gonna surely break my heart of gold...
Seven A-M, Billy! Time to wake up and face a brand new day!

(BILLY, *dressed in a large sleeper onesie, sits up. He yawns, stretches his arms, smiles.*)

BILLY: Good morning, Mommy!

CLAIRE: Good morning, little Billy boo-boo. Guess what we have for breakfast?

BILLY: Oatmeal!

CLAIRE: Is it oatmeal? I don't know...

BILLY: Oatmeal! Oatmeal?!

CLAIRE: Well, let's see... It's hot...it's drippy...

BILLY: Oatmeal!

CLAIRE: Oh, no...I think it's soggy corn flakes.

(BILLY*'s face draws into a disappointed frown.*)

CLAIRE: Nooo...it's oatmeal!

BILLY: Yayy!

(CLAIRE *gives* BILLY *the oatmeal bowl, which is devoured in one long gulp.*)

BILLY: More!

CLAIRE: Well, Billy, you know what happens when you eat too fast.

BILLY: Fwow up?

CLAIRE: Let's just see how that bowl sits in your tummy before I get you another.

BILLY: Still hungry!

CLAIRE: Mommy has to go to work now. Maybe Jane will get you some more.

BILLY: Still hungry!

CLAIRE: Why don't you count to five minutes and then we'll see. Just look at the clock on the wall and count five minutes.

BILLY: Can we play the game for five minutes?

CLAIRE: Mommy has to finish getting ready for work.

BILLY: But I wanna play the game! I wanna play the game!

CLAIRE: Billy, Mommy has to / get ready.

BILLY: Play game! Play game!

CLAIRE: Okay, Billy.

(BILLY *runs to window*)

BILLY: Come on, Mommy! Come on!

(CLAIRE *follows* BILLY *and sits by window.*)

CLAIRE: Okay, Billy. Here we go. I spy with my little eye...something that begins with T.

BILLY: I spy with my little eye...umm...a tree!

CLAIRE: And what do we say about trees?

BILLY: Trees have leaves and trees have bark
Lots of trees live in the park
With lots of birds all gray and red
That make filthy poop on Billy's head!

CLAIRE: That's right, Billy, bird poop is icky filthy yuck.

BILLY: More! More!

CLAIRE: I spy with my little eye...something that begins with D!

BILLY: I spy with my little eye...something that begins with...doggie!

CLAIRE: And doggies...?

BILLY: "Doggies have hair and carry fleas
And pee on fire plugs and big tall trees
They have big sharp teeth you should take note
Just waiting to tear out Billy's throat!"
I'm glad we don't have a doggie.

CLAIRE: Doggies are dangerous, Billy. They look all nice and friendly, but they're really vicious. Mommy has to finish / getting ready for work.

BILLY: One more! One more! Please!!

CLAIRE: All right, Billy. Last one. I spy with my little eye...something that begins with C!

BILLY: I spy with my little eye...something that begins with...car!

CLAIRE: And what do cars do?

BILLY: "Cars go vroom and cars go fast;
As you can see when they go past;
You should never walk into the street;
'cause cars will mash you into bloody meat."

*(SFX: Car horn from outside window)*

BILLY: Honk, honk! Honk, honk! Car horn!

CLAIRE: That's right. It's a car horn.

BILLY: Honk! Honk! Wanna go for a car ride!

CLAIRE: Whoa, no car rides for Billy. What did we just say?

BILLY: But I wanna go inside the car! I wanna honk the horn!

CLAIRE: Car rides are dangerous, Billy. Remember what Mommy told you?

BILLY: I wanna honk the horn!

CLAIRE: You have your own car horn, don't you?

BILLY: I want a real car horn!

CLAIRE: Here, honk *your* car horn. *(Brings toy, exits to kitchen)*

BILLY: *(Honks the feeble squeak toy. Gets bored, throws toy)* This sucks.

CLAIRE: *(On re-entry)* What kind of word is that? Where did you learn that language?

BILLY: I don't know.

CLAIRE: You learned that somewhere. Where did you learn it?

BILLY: I don't know!!

CLAIRE: I should wash your mouth out with soap, Billy. You want me to do that?

BILLY: No!

CLAIRE: Where did you hear that? Was that from babysitter Jane?

BILLY: No! Babysitter Jane never says bad words!

CLAIRE: Then where did you hear it? I'm getting the soap!

BILLY: No! No soap!

CLAIRE: Where did you hear that?

BILLY: I heard it…I heard it…out the window!

CLAIRE: You heard it out the window?

BILLY: From Mr Scary Man with the Paper Bag!

CLAIRE: What were you doing listening at the window? You know the window is supposed to be closed when Mommy's not home. Do you remember why the window is always closed?

BILLY: Because Billy could fall out and smash his head open and his brains will leak out all over the sidewalk.

CLAIRE: That's right. So no more open window and no more listening to Mr Scary Man with the Paper Bag, is that clear? Billy?

BILLY: I made a poopy.

CLAIRE: Well, then we'll just clean you up. Billy made poopy. Billy's oatmeal goes in one end…

BILLY: And out the other! Oatmeal goes into Billy and comes out poopy!

CLAIRE: Go to your crib and I'll get you a new diaper. *(He exits offstage.)* And no finger painting with poopies!

*(Apartment door opens, babysitter* JANE *enters.)*

BILLY: Babysitter Jane! Mommy, babysitter Jane is here!

CLAIRE: *(O S)* I'll be there in just a second!

JANE: Good morning, Billy!

BILLY: Good morning! How are you today?

JANE: I'm just fine, Billy. Are you looking forward to us spending the day together?

BILLY: Mommy's getting me a new diaper. 'Cause I made poopy in mine.

(CLAIRE *enters.*)

CLAIRE: Good morning, Jane. How are you today?

JANE: I'm just fine, Claire. And you?

CLAIRE: Fine as a frog's hair. And running late for work. *(Gives* JANE *the diaper)* Take care of this for me? Thanks.

(CLAIRE *crosses to front door; maybe he dons a coat, maybe not. How cold is it where you are?*)

CLAIRE: I don't know if it's me or not, but it seems like we use fewer diapers on the days when you're here? How often do you change Billy?

JANE: How often? I don't know. I don't count.

CLAIRE: Guess for me.

JANE: Two, maybe three times. More when you give him oatmeal for breakfast.

CLAIRE: Well, it certainly seems strange. It seemed Monday he didn't poop at all. Never mind. Just keep an eye on his backside, okay? We don't want a pileup, do we?

JANE: Of course not, Claire. No problem.

CLAIRE: Good. Like I said, it's probably the wind blowing through the trees of my mind. Now you have a good day, Billy.

BILLY: I will!

CLAIRE: I love you!

BILLY: I love you too, Mommy!

CLAIRE: I'm going to miss you.

BILLY: I'll miss you, too!

CLAIRE: Oh, and Jane…

JANE: Yes?

CLAIRE: I'm sure I'm mistaking it, but you don't ever smoke in the apartment, do you?

JANE: Of course not!

CLAIRE: Because normally I can smell it on your clothes. I don't particularly mind it; it's impossible not to reek of tobacco when you smoke, but I thought there had been a stronger than normal smell the last few times.

JANE: I can assure you, Claire, that I do not smoke here.

CLAIRE: Good. Well I'm just a mass of worries today, it seems. Between the poop question, the smoking stench, and the new strange and somewhat vulgar words coming out of Billy's mouth, which I'm sure he did not hear from you, well, I'm just at a loss for explanations. I just hope it's not going to be one of those days.

JANE: You have nothing to worry about, Claire. I assure you—

CLAIRE: Yes, I'm sure. And I'm not worried. Just running late, that's all. Well, Billy, you be a good boy and I'll see you tonight at dinner.

BILLY: Bye, Mommy!

(CLAIRE *exits.* JANE *goes to the window and watches.* BILLY *scrambles out of his crib and joins her.*)

JANE: And there he goes, out the front door…down the street…and down the subway entrance. Hallelujah.

BILLY: I still have a poopy in my diaper.

JANE: Here's another diaper. Go change.

BILLY: But Mommy…

JANE: Mommy changes you. I know. Do you want to be a big boy? Big boys change themselves.

BILLY: I know. And big boys go on the big boy potty. I forgot again.

(BILLY *exits to bathroom with diaper.* JANE *quickly lights a cigarette, blowing the smoke out the window. She stays at the window.)*

JANE: *(Sotto voce)* It's worth it. It's worth it, Jane. Whatever it takes, it's worth it. We're almost there. *(Normal voice, to* BILLY *O S)* Billy?

BILLY: Yeah?

JANE: Have you decided about going outside yet?

BILLY: No…

JANE: *(Sotto voce)* You wait much longer and I'll be in diapers, too. *(Normal voice)* Billy! You've had weeks to think about it.

(BILLY *reenters;* JANE *hurriedly drops cigarette out window.)*

BILLY: Mommy says it's too dangerous for little boys.

JANE: Billy, isn't this what you've been telling me you've wanted? "I wanna go see the world." "I wanna play with other little boys."

BILLY: Yeah, I do, but…

JANE: Then there's only one way to do it. They aren't going to come up here. You have to go to them.

BILLY: But Mommy—

JANE: And we have to get Mommy to agree to it. Somehow. I'm on your side, Billy.

BILLY: I like the way you smell.

JANE: And I like your smell, too, Billy. Except when you have poop in your drawers.

BILLY: That's my diaper. *(He holds up the used diaper.)*

JANE: And what do we do with used diapers?

BILLY: We put them in the diaper bin. *(He puts diaper in the bin.)*

BILLY: Can I have a cigarette?

JANE: No, Billy.

BILLY: Big boys smoke cigarettes. I've seen them out the window.

JANE: Smoking cigarettes is stupid.

BILLY: You do it.

JANE: I know. I'm stupid.

BILLY: You're not stupid! You're smart! You go to college! You talk to lots of professors.

JANE: No, Billy, I'm not stupid. But people don't always make the right decision. We make mistakes and I did a bad, stupid thing when I started smoking. I wasn't thinking ahead, Billy, like I should have been. But thank you for saying I'm smart. You're really very sweet. And because I like you very much, I'm not giving you one.

(BILLY *tries to argue.*)

JANE: So stop asking.

BILLY: Okay.

JANE: So, what shall we do? Tell some more stories?

BILLY: Unh-uh. No more stories.

JANE: Why not?

BILLY: Because remember you told me a story about Mr Scary Man with the Paper Bag? And he…he…talks to people only he can see?

JANE: Yes, and what about it?

BILLY: I was looking out the window yesterday and he was screaming! He was in the middle of the street and he was screaming at some little boys.

JANE: Oh, sh—. Brother.

BILLY: And he was really scary.

JANE: Well, Billy, he—

BILLY: And then he threw his paper bag at them and it broke and then he went into the alley and made pee-pee against the wall!

JANE: And Claire let you see that?

BILLY: Yeah, he was making me watch.

JANE: He was making you watch?

BILLY: And he told me that man was crazy and he likes to hurt little boys.

JANE: Did you tell Claire that I told you a story about him?

BILLY: No…

JANE: Because our stories are just for ourselves, right? I haven't told anyone the stories you tell me. It's our little secret. If you go telling our stories, then maybe Claire wouldn't like it.

BILLY: Why not?

JANE: Because Claire, well, …might not understand that you and I are sharing secrets. Little secrets. Well, why don't we continue with our special project?

(JANE *digs out a small handheld camera.*)

BILLY: How come I always have to talk to the camera?

JANE: You know why. You talk to the camera, we continue making the All About Billy Book. And then I let you watch yourself telling the story. Don't you like it? Isn't it fun?

BILLY: I guess so. Umm…

JANE: Yes?

BILLY: Can I…never mind.

JANE: What is it, Billy?

BILLY: Nothing.

JANE: Billy, come on. Tell me what it is. You can tell me.

BILLY: Can I touch you?

JANE: Billy…

BILLY: Just a little?

JANE: I really want to play this game first, Billy. Just let me ask you a few questions and then we can watch Billy on the T-V. Won't that be cool?

BILLY: I wanna touch you.

JANE: I understand why you want to; boys your age start getting these desires, but touching someone else is a very private and personal thing, Billy. People have to be very, very good friends to do that.

BILLY: But we're good friends! You're my best friend!

JANE: Well, Billy, I'm flattered…

BILLY: I mean I don't know anybody else, so that makes you my best friend.

JANE: I know that, Billy, but we're not…that kind of friends. It's different.

BILLY: Why?

JANE: Well…

BILLY: I love you.

JANE: You…what?

BILLY: I love you!

JANE: Oh, god. No, Billy, you don't.

BILLY: Yes I do. I love you! And I would like to marry you!

JANE: You want to…Billy, you are way too young to marry anyone. You are still a little boy.

BILLY: No, I'm not! Look—my weenie is standing straight up! Look!

JANE: Billy! No! Put that away! Right now!

BILLY: But Mr Scary Man with the Paper Bag shows *his* weenie to people!

JANE: Mr Scary Man...he...holy freakin' jesus... Look, Billy. Mr Scary Man with the Paper Bag...is sick. He's sick. He doesn't really know where he is a lot of the time. He thinks he's in a special world, and only he can see it. He gets confused a lot, Billy. And he does things that are okay in his world, but aren't in this one.

(BILLY *starts to cry.*)

JANE: Now, Billy...

BILLY: I did something bad!

JANE: No, Billy, no, you didn't do anything bad. You just think that it's okay to show your...weenie...to people, and really...it's a very private thing. We don't do that. Normally.

BILLY: Will I grow up to be like Mr Scary Man with the Paper Bag because I showed you my weenie?

JANE: Of course not, Billy. No. Mr Scary Man...he's sick, Billy. Very sick. And you're not. You're not, okay?

BILLY: Do you still like me?

JANE: Of course, Billy. I will always like you.

BILLY: Always?

JANE: You will always be my very, very special friend.

BILLY: But not the kind of friend I can show my weenie to?

JANE: No, Billy. Now. How about we get some more work done on All About Billy?

BILLY: I don't want to.

JANE: But we've come so far already! We are so close to finishing! It's almost done!

BILLY: Will Mommy read it?

JANE: He can if you want him to. Do you want him to?

BILLY: I don't know.

JANE: Well, if you want him to, I'll get him his very own copy. And we can both sign it to…make it just like you!

BILLY: Like me?

JANE: That's right. What did we say you were? Very, very…

BILLY & JANE: Special.

JANE: That's right. Very, very special.

BILLY: I…

JANE: Come on now, Billy. Think. Is this really important to you? Remember we talked about how important is it to you to finish this?

BILLY: …okay.

JANE: That's my very special Billy! Now close your eyes…go ahead…that's good…and remember. Try to concentrate on your breathing…just listen to your breaths…nice and slow…that's it…nice and easy… Now picture your magic pond in your mind. Your pond is very calm. It's quiet, Billy. Very quiet. You are getting closer to the pond. The water is warm, just like a bath. You get closer…closer. Are you ready to go under?

(BILLY *nods slightly.*)

JANE: Then slowly put your face beneath the surface, Billy. I want you to think back, Billy, think back to when you were just a little baby…and tell me what happened to your real Mommy. Don't cry! It's okay!

Nobody will hurt you, Billy. Nobody will hurt you when I'm around. I'm going to watch out for you and nothing bad will ever get through. Trust me, Billy. Now tell me what happened to your mom.

BILLY: I see pretty lights.

JANE: What kind of lights? What colors?

BILLY: Red ones. Blue ones. Red ones.

JANE: And what else?

BILLY: A bad smell.

JANE: What kind of smell, Billy?

BILLY: Bad smell. Hurts my nose. It burns my eyes!

JANE: What does it smell like, Billy? Have you smelled it before?

BILLY: It stings! My eyes hurt!

JANE: I'm right here, Billy. I'm protecting you. Tell me more about it. Where is Mommy?

BILLY: I don't know…I don't know…

JANE: Try and tell me what's happening. Tell me about the lights…

BILLY: Pretty. Lots of lights. I'm being carried.

JANE: Who's carrying you?

BILLY: It's white. It's all white.

JANE: What's white, Billy? Where is it white?

BILLY: I'm being carried…it's white…

(SFX: JANE's cell phone; BILLY is startled.)

JANE: *Fuck!*

BILLY: Aaaah!

(BILLY grabs JANE in fright, holds her close, almost suffocating her.)

JANE: It's okay, Billy. I have you, I have you. I'm right here. There's no need to be frightened. It was just a noise.... You're safe.

(JANE *turns into him, facing upstage, puts her arms around him.* BILLY *holds her around the waist tightly. His head moves down.*)

JANE: Billy? No, Billy! No! What are you...omigod... Billy. ...Oh, god...Billy....Billy, don't...omigod...oh god, Billy...shhh, it's okay, it's okay...

(*Lights fade to black.*)

## Scene II

(BILLY *enters, laughing, from bathroom;* CLAIRE *behind, buttoning up back of his onesy*)

CLAIRE: Slow down, big boy! Mommy has to make sure your poopie flap is all closed up.

(BILLY *continues to walk around the room,* CLAIRE *behind, like a "whip" effect.*)

CLAIRE: Slow down, Billy!

BILLY: I'm an airplane!

CLAIRE: The airplane better slow down or all the baggage will drop out the back end! Whoa, there goes someone's suitcase! Whoa! Oh no! I think that was someone's golf clubs! There they go!

(CLAIRE *finally gets* BILLY *buttoned up.*)

CLAIRE: Now Billy the airplane has to make a landing! Ready?

BILLY: I'm landing! Watch out!

CLAIRE: Here comes Billy!

(CLAIRE *makes airplane sound as* BILLY *revolves, then sits D C*)

BILLY: Airplane needs food, Mommy! Or it can't fly.

CLAIRE: Airplane needs to have its hair dried and its beard trimmed first, or it'll be a very hairy airplane flying around. *(Begins drying* BILLY's *hair. At one point the towel covers* BILLY's *face)* Uh-oh! Where did Billy go?

*(*BILLY *giggles.)*

CLAIRE: I can't find Billy! Where did my little airplane go? *(Lifts up the front of towel)* There you are!

*(A bit of improv: peekaboo with towel)*

CLAIRE: There you are, now, all nice and dry. Now settle down because Mommy has to trim that bushy great beard of yours. Airplanes have to fly smoothly, without lots of hair sticking out all over the place. Mommy has the scissors, so be careful and don't move that head of yours. *Billy!*

*(*BILLY *turns and gives* CLAIRE *a big hug)*

BILLY: I love you, Mommy.

CLAIRE: *(Hugging back)* And I love you too, Billy. But you have to stay still, or Mommy may accidentally stick the scissors in your eyeball, okay?

*(*CLAIRE *begins trimming* BILLY's *beard.)*

BILLY: Okay. What's for dinner tonight?

CLAIRE: Fish.

*(*BILLY *makes face.)*

CLAIRE: It's good for you. It's brain food.

BILLY: Will it make me big and strong?

CLAIRE: If you eat it all it will. Fish is good for making little boys into big, strong, healthy boys.

BILLY: Will I always be a boy?

CLAIRE: You will always be my boy. And you know what that means.

BILLY: It means you will always be my Mommy!

CLAIRE: On the little red nosie, Billy-baby-boo-boo.

BILLY: Mommy?

CLAIRE: Yes, my darling?

BILLY: When will I be big enough?

CLAIRE: Big enough for what?

BILLY: Go outside.

CLAIRE: Why would you want to go outside? Didn't we talk about that? Outside is dangerous! You don't want to go outside.

BILLY: Yes I do.

CLAIRE: No, you don't.

BILLY: Yes I do.

CLAIRE: No, you don't.

BILLY: Yes I do.

CLAIRE: No, you don't.

BILLY: I wanna go outside and play with other boys!

CLAIRE: Outside is no place for little boys. Even big boys get hurt. Why on earth would you want to go outside after all we've talked about? You know what's out there, Billy. Tell me, Billy. Tell me.

BILLY: Doggies…

CLAIRE: That's right. And what else?

BILLY: I just wanted to…

CLAIRE: What else, Billy?

BILLY: I see other little boys—

CLAIRE: Tell me what else is out there, Billy. No dinner until you do.

BILLY: But I…I just wanna…

CLAIRE: What else is out there besides mean, vicious doggies? I can wait here all night.

BILLY: I don't care what else is out there. I wanna be a big boy!

CLAIRE: Why all of a sudden do you want to go outside?

BILLY: I don't know.

CLAIRE: Remember a long time ago? When you were smaller? I tried to take you outside and you screamed and cried and kicked so badly? I had to take you right back upstairs.

BILLY: I know, but…

CLAIRE: You were so scared of leaving the apartment I didn't know what to do.

BILLY: I just…wanna…because…

CLAIRE: Are you hiding things from Mommy? You know what happens to little boys who keep secrets from their mommies.

BILLY: No…

CLAIRE: Their brains start to expand…and get bigger because of all the things they never tell mommy. Pretty soon they'll have a head that's too big for their beds.

BILLY: My head's not getting any bigger! It's not!

CLAIRE: My goodness, the things I'm finding in your beard! I really should trim you more often. Anything could be in here! And if your head gets bigger I'm going to have to buy a lawn mower and make you lie down on the floor.

(BILLY *giggles*)

CLAIRE: I'll just fire up the motor and get those sharp blades spinning and run that lawn mower over your head several times. And that will keep your beard nice and trimmed. Vroom! Vroom! There goes Billy's beard! It's a good thing you don't have any secrets or I'll have to get a really, really big lawnmower.

BILLY: I don't want a lawnmower on my face.

CLAIRE: I don't know, Billy. Now if you're sure you have no secrets—

BILLY: I don't!

CLAIRE: Because the bigger the secret, the bigger your head will get. Bigger…and bigger…and bigger.

BILLY: Will it 'splode?

CLAIRE: I don't know. It just might. It would have to be a really big, nasty secret. Now there. We're all done. Are you ready for dinner?

BILLY: Yes, Mommy.

CLAIRE: Then I'll just go finish cooking.

(BILLY *gets up.*)

BILLY: I love you, Mommy.

(BILLY *turns, picks up* CLAIRE, *gives bone-crunching hug.*)

CLAIRE: I love you, too.

(CLAIRE *extricates himself and exits to kitchen.* BILLY *looks after him, waits until* CLAIRE *is safely cooking, then reaches under the blanket in the crib and pulls out a cigarette. He sniffs it, then tosses it out the window.* BILLY *crosses to kitchen and exits.*)

## Scene III

(*During the scene,* CLAIRE *will replace batteries in five smoke detectors.*)

JANE: Claire, I'm not understanding any of this.

CLAIRE: Perhaps you haven't been listening. I'm telling you in the plainest words I know. Billy, my baby boy, is getting these very strange ideas in his head.

JANE: Oh, come on, Claire / this is ridiculous.

CLAIRE: Ideas about leaving his home. His home! Where he is safe.

JANE: Safe? Claire, he's a captive!

CLAIRE: A captive? So then what does that make me? His kidnapper? Are you accusing me / of kidnapping my own baby?

JANE: Claire, you are being silly. / I only want what's best...

CLAIRE: I will not be called names in my own home!

JANE: Can I help you with those?

CLAIRE: Thank you but no.

JANE: Are you sure? You certainly have quite a few of them.

CLAIRE: I do not take chances when it comes to Billy. My baby boy needs extra special care.

JANE: I agree with you. Billy does need special care. And...Claire...as long as we're talking about that, do you really think it's okay for him to stay in this apartment as long as he does? He really should be going out.

CLAIRE: Are you his mommy?

JANE: Of course not, Claire.

CLAIRE: Well, I am his mommy. I take care of him, and I know what's best for him. And if you can't see that, then maybe you should not be caring for him. I'm starting to have doubts about you lately.

JANE: What? What doubts could you possibly have?

CLAIRE: Billy is getting these ideas about leaving here from *some*place, Jane. They're not invented. They're not just springing out of his head on their own.

JANE: Yes, they are, Claire! He wants to go outside! He's never been outside. He looks at it every day. For hours. He needs to explore. He's what, thirty years old?

CLAIRE: Billy is three years old.

JANE: Claire, there isn't another three-year-old in the world that needs his beard cut once a week. Claire, come on. I'm not fighting you; I'm trying to look out for him, that's all.

CLAIRE: Billy is three years old.

JANE: Yes. He is. He is three years old. He poops his pants, he can't dress himself, he cries at the smallest thing. But I'll tell you something and you're not gonna like it. Billy knows he's not three years old. He knows you know it, too.

CLAIRE: Keep your voice down!

JANE: Sorry. Why is he in your room?

CLAIRE: Because he came into Mommy's bed crying in the middle of the night. Icky nasty dreams.

JANE: He hasn't told me that. Does it happen often?

CLAIRE: Lately. I'm sure I don't know what it's all about. You're not telling him scary stories, are you?

JANE: No. And I don't let him watch Mr Scary Man with the Paper Bag, either.

CLAIRE: Well…I'm sure…

JANE: If you really want what's best for him, you ought to start getting him out of the house.

CLAIRE: Don't you presume to tell me how to raise my child. Don't you dare! I should fire you.

JANE: You need to think twice about that.

CLAIRE: Excuse me?

JANE: Think, Claire. How many babysitters have you been through? I've been here over a year, four days a week. No one has stayed but me. I am just simply telling you the truth. Have I ever—ever—asked *any*thing of you? Much as you might hate to admit it, you do need me. Billy is very important to me. I care about him. A lot. And he needs me, too.

CLAIRE: And I thought Billy had an overactive imagination! Are you saying he can't do without you? / My god, the arrogance!

JANE: Cut it out, Claire. You know he needs me. He cannot survive here without a babysitter. You want to try breaking in a new sitter? Remember how long it took before he stopped going into major fits when you left the house? He waits at that window every day starting at five twenty-five and never takes his eyes off that subway entrance, waiting for you to come out at five thirty, look up and wave at him.

BILLY: Because he's my baby and he loves me!

JANE: Because he thinks if he's not there you won't find your way home! How will Mommy know which apartment to go to if he doesn't see Billy at the window?

CLAIRE: That is complete nonsense! He loves me and can't wait for me to get home.

JANE: He thinks that one of these days you're going to go to work and won't come back.

CLAIRE: Rubbish! You called him a captive. You think—

JANE: He is, Claire! He is! He's a captive who is scared to death to go outside, so he stays here and pretends he's still a three-year-old. What are you gonna do in five years? Ten? What if something happens to you? Where will he go? What will he do?

CLAIRE: You seem to think I'm some kind of evil witch—

JANE: / Absolutely not, Claire.

CLAIRE: —like something out of a fairy tale. Well, I'm not. I am a single mother keeping my baby boy safe and sound.

BILLY: *(O S)* Mommy?

JANE: All I'm suggesting is that maybe we can work together on this. I really do care about Billy. I am not trying to fight you.

BILLY: *(O S)* Mommy?

CLAIRE: Raising a child is no afternoon flight in the clouds. Keeping him from harm is my biggest worry. I'm just doing the best I know how.

## Scene IV

(BILLY *is at the window, watching. While he watches he holds his hands open and puts his thumbs in the middle of his forehead, stretching his fingers around the sides.*)

JANE: *(O S)* Do you see him yet, Billy?

(BILLY *looks up at the clock.*)

BILLY: It's not time yet! He still has five minutes.

(JANE *enters.*)

JANE: Well, I have to leave when he gets home and you still haven't told me why you wanted me to bring a tape measure.

BILLY: Umm…I want you to measure my head.

JANE: Measure …? What?

BILLY: I need to know how big my head is.

JANE: Okay… Why do you want to know how big your head is?

BILLY: Because.

JANE: "Because." There's got to be a better reason than "because".

BILLY: No there doesn't. Because.

JANE: You just want to know how big your head is. Do you want to know what hat size you are?

BILLY: Yes.

JANE: What kind of hat do you want?

BILLY: I don't know.

JANE: Then why do you want to know your hat size?

BILLY: Because. I want to know how big my head is.

JANE: Whatever. Hold still.

(JANE *measures* BILLY's *head.*)

JANE: *(True size of actor's head)* inches.

BILLY: I want you to measure my head every time.

JANE: Every time? Are you expecting your head to grow? Or shrink?

BILLY: I just wanna know.

JANE: Billy, I will be happy to measure your head, but I'd like to know why.

BILLY: Just because.

JANE: Let me guess, Billy. Did Claire tell you to measure your head?

BILLY: No.

JANE: Billy? You can't hide from me, Billy. What did Claire tell you about your head?

BILLY: Mommy said…that every secret I keep stays in my head and makes it grow bigger.

JANE: He said your head would grow bigger because of secrets?

BILLY: He said if I was keeping secrets then my head would grow so big I'd look like a basketball on a pencil.

JANE: Did you tell him you have a secret?

BILLY: No!

JANE: Billy, I'm not going to get angry or upset with you. Are you sure you didn't say anything about our little project?

BILLY: I didn't say nothing! I didn't say nothing! I didn't / say nothing!

JANE: Okay, Billy. It's all right. I believe you.

BILLY: I didn't say nothing.

JANE: Okay, Billy. I believe you. It's okay. You know, we're almost done with the book. Aren't you excited? All I need from you are a few more details and then I will finish writing the book and put in the pictures I took and it will be all done.

BILLY: I don't care.

JANE: But it's so much fun, Billy.

BILLY: I don't wanna see myself on the T-V. I don't wanna have my own Billy T-V Show anymore.

JANE: Billy, when I complete my thesis, lots of people are going to want to meet you and talk to you and take their pictures with you. You're going to be famous the world over. This is going to be big, Billy. Nobody will have seen anything like this before, and both you and

I are going to be on T-V. People will write books about you and me.

BILLY: Why will they write books about you? I thought the thee...what you said was all about me.

JANE: "Thesis", Billy. It's something you write about somebody or something, and it's all about them. Lots and lots of pages and pictures. And I'll be famous, too, because I wrote the first book all about Billy. I'll get my degree with lots of honors, and I'll get a great job. This is a once-in-a-lifetime chance for both of us. Don't you want us to be famous?

BILLY: I don't care.

JANE: Is something wrong? Do you want to talk to me about something?

BILLY: I told you. I wanna touch you.

JANE: And I told you that we aren't those kinds of friends, Billy. You have to find someone else to be a special friend.

BILLY: Do you have a special friend?

JANE: Well...yes. Yes, I do.

BILLY: I don't wanna talk to you no more. I want Mommy to come home. I'm not talking to you anymore.

JANE: But Billy...look...

(BILLY *resumes looking out the window.*)

BILLY: I spy with my little eye...

JANE: Billy. Billy!

BILLY: I have to look out the window!

JANE: Billy...

BILLY: If I don't look out the window, then Mommy can't find his way home!

JANE: Okay, Billy…

BILLY: Mommy needs to find his way home! He'll get lost and disappear! He'll go away and nobody will ever find him again!

JANE: Claire can find his way home, Billy. He's a big girl.

BILLY: He needs to see me in the window!

JANE: Okay, Billy. Just keep looking out the window. I can film you while you / watch for Mommy.

BILLY: No! No more camera!

JANE: But Billy…

BILLY: No camera! No camera!

JANE: Billy, it's all right, / it's all right!

BILLY: No camera! No camera!

JANE: *All right, Billy!* I'm putting the camera away!

BILLY: I want you to go and never come back.

JANE: I think you're just a little upset.

BILLY: You keep asking me to do things and tell you stories, and I don't get nothing!

JANE: What do you want?

BILLY: I wanna touch you.

JANE: I told you: I can't let you do that.

BILLY: I'm not playing with you no more. I hate you. I'm gonna tell.

JANE: Billy. Shit. William. Telling tales is wrong. Telling secrets is a bad thing.

BILLY: I don't care. I have to watch for Mommy. And when Mommy gets home I'm gonna tell him…

JANE: William, you have to / try and calm down…

BILLY: And he's gonna make you go away! Go away and never come back! There he is! Hi, Mommy! Hi, Mommy!

JANE: William? William! OKAY!

BILLY: What?

JANE: Sit down, face me, and put your hands in your lap.

BILLY: Why?

JANE: Because.

BILLY: Why?

JANE: Because I said so!

BILLY: But…

JANE: Do what I tell you!

(BILLY *puts his hands in his lap.*)

JANE: Put your hands down further and keep your legs tight against each other. Do it, Billy. Good. Now don't move!

(JANE *leans forward and kisses him.* BILLY *squirms, clearly excited. He reaches for her, but she pulls away.*)

BILLY: More!

JANE: That's enough, Billy.

BILLY: More!

JANE: No, Billy! That's enough. Now go to the door and wait for Mommy.

BILLY: I liked it.

JANE: I'm glad. Now remember: This is part of our private deal. You don't tell anyone, right?

BILLY: Okay! Okay! (*Starts to move toward apartment door, then stops*) I made poopy!

(JANE *gestures toward bathroom.* BILLY *exits to bathroom.*)

JANE: Omigod. I am so going to hell.

## Scene V

(CLAIRE *knits, looking on while* BILLY *lies on the floor and turns the pages of his coloring book*)

BILLY: And that one is Mommy, too!

CLAIRE: You've been so busy! And so many pictures of Mommy! Why does Mommy have worms on his face?

BILLY: (*Giggling*) That's Mommy in the morning before he shaves.

CLAIRE: Oh, is it, really? You're quite the portrait artist, aren't you? And is this one Mommy, too? But with… my goodness…

BILLY: No. That's not Mommy. That's Babysitter Jane!

CLAIRE: Oh, yes. I can see that. That's her hair. And those are her glasses. And…these…Well, this is somewhat overstated, don't you think?

BILLY: Thank you for my new crayons, Mommy.

CLAIRE: You're welcome, Billy baby-boo-boo. (*Points to book*) And what's that?

BILLY: This is our apartment building. And that's me in the window, waving at you so you can find your way home!

CLAIRE: Oh, Billy, I can find my way home, it's only… well… And why are there people all over the street?

BILLY: Because everybody likes Billy and wants to visit him!

CLAIRE: That's a lot of people, isn't it?

BILLY: And I wave at them from the window.

CLAIRE: And why did they come to Billy's house?

BILLY: Because Billy was famous! And everybody liked him!

CLAIRE: And why was Billy famous?

BILLY: *(Thinks)* I don't know.

CLAIRE: Well, Billy must have done something wonderful! Maybe he becomes a famous artist! And people from all over come to see his drawings!

BILLY: And they make him a thesis!

CLAIRE: That sounds like a babysitter Jane word. Was she talking about her big project for grad school?

BILLY: I guess so.

CLAIRE: I'm sure that must have been it. Little pitchers have big ears, you know!

*(Clock SFX: "It's 8 P-M! Farmer Bob must tuck in all the animals nice and tight!")*

CLAIRE: You know what that means!

BILLY: Okay. *(He walks toward his crib.)*

CLAIRE: Billy? Are you forgetting something? No bed until you brush your teeth.

BILLY: Okay.

*(BILLY exits to bathroom. CLAIRE picks up the drawing of BILLY at the window and looks at it. BILLY returns with toothbrush, toothpaste and bowl on tray.)*

CLAIRE: Maybe we should get you a new toothbrush. This one looks like Spiderman has been through the wringer. What kind would you like? Another Spiderman?

BILLY: A Billy toothbrush.

CLAIRE: I don't think they make Billy toothbrushes.

BILLY: They will when I'm famous.

*(CLAIRE begins brushing BILLY's teeth.)*

CLAIRE: Open wide! You're pretty certain that you're going to be famous, aren't you?

BILLY: *(With a toothbrush in his mouth)* The world over.

CLAIRE: My goodness, what elegant phrases you're learning! And how do you know this? Did you have a dream? Did Billy dream all this up at naptime?

BILLY: Uh-uh. It's real!

CLAIRE: I'm sure it is. Then I guess we'll have to get you some new clothes. You must have nice new clothes to meet new people. And we'll have to brush your teeth extra special. We don't want people to see you with dirty teeth. Oh! If you're going to be famous, then maybe you'll be on T-V! Wouldn't that be wonderful?

BILLY: It's okay.

CLAIRE: "Okay?" Billy, being on T-V is very, very special! You'd have to look nice!

BILLY: I just go on in my diaper.

CLAIRE: Well, then it would have to be a very special diaper.

BILLY: And then I could get a bike and go outside and play, right?

CLAIRE: A bike? On these streets?

BILLY: If I was famous it would mean I was grown up!

CLAIRE: We have had this conversation before, Billy. You are pushing Mommy's patience. You may not have a bike.

BILLY: But if I was famous I…I would need a bike!

CLAIRE: And what would you need a bike for?

BILLY: Because…because…then I could go visit Mommy!

CLAIRE: What?

BILLY: I wanna visit Mommy!

CLAIRE: Billy, I'm your Mommy.

BILLY: You're not really Mommy! You're Claire-Mommy pretending to be Mommy because Mommy went away! I want Mommy-Mommy!

CLAIRE: I am the only Mommy you have, Billy. Now—

BILLY: I wanna go inna car and go to Mommy's house! I wanna honk the horn! Honk, honk!

CLAIRE: There is no other Mommy! And there is no other house!

BILLY: Mommy lives…Mommy lives…

CLAIRE: Billy!

BILLY: I want Mommy to come back!

CLAIRE: There is no other mommy, Billy! Now listen to me—

BILLY: Why doesn't she come back? Was I bad?

CLAIRE: She's not coming back because— (*Sotto voce*) Goddammit! (*Normal voice*) You want to know why she doesn't come back? Because she's not a real mommy. She's not a good mommy, Billy. I'm Mommy. Understand? I'm Mommy, and I'm taking care of you. I. AM. MOMMY. Look at me! I have an apron, and I cook your food because that's what good mommies do. I have little glasses to read you stories. I knit because all mommies do that. I have lots of diapers to change your poo-poos. I have all mommy clothes because mommies have to wear special clothes to cook and clean and tidy up Billy's room.

(BILLY's *crying intensifies*.)

BILLY: I wanna go see Mommy! I miss Mommy!

CLAIRE: Why do you want to find her all of a sudden? Did babysitter Jane tell you / to go find her?

BILLY: No! She didn't say nothing. She didn't...

CLAIRE: Billy, I want you to listen to me. Are you listening?

BILLY: Yes.

CLAIRE: Yes WHAT?

BILLY: Yes, Mommy!

CLAIRE: Good. Now we cannot go find...Mommy-Mommy, because she went away. She went far, far away, and nobody knows where she went.

BILLY: There was an accident, and Mommy got sick.

CLAIRE: Where did you hear that? Billy? Answer me now. / Where did you hear that?

BILLY: I remember it. I remember the pretty colored lights and it was all white. And I was scared! And they took Mommy away and she was sick. And they didn't bring Mommy back! They took Mommy!

CLAIRE: Billy, how can you remember that?

BILLY: I dream it. Lots. 'S why I can't sleep because the dreams come and scare me. That's why I don't wanna get sick. It will go all white and they will come and take me away and they'll put me inna hospital and they'll throw away the key! And you won't be able to find me!
Hospitals are big and white;
With ambulances and flashing lights;

CLAIRE: Billy! STOP IT!

BILLY: The doctors' knives go snip and cut;
Then they rip out Billy's guts!
I don't wanna go to a hospital!

CLAIRE: No one will come to take you away. No one. I'm here, and I'm taking care of you. Now I have to ask you a question. So sit still. You're my good boy. Now

I want you to answer me, and I want the truth, do you
understand? Billy, do you understand?

BILLY: I unnerstan'...

CLAIRE: Now Billy, listen to me very carefully. Did you
tell any of this to babysitter Jane?

BILLY: No.

CLAIRE: Are you sure? Think hard! Think very hard!

BILLY: No.

CLAIRE: Because if you did, she may tell the doctors.
And then they will come and take you away from me.

BILLY: No...I don't want to go away...

CLAIRE: Then you have to trust Mommy. Trust
Mommy and no one else. Do you trust Mommy?

BILLY: Yes...

CLAIRE: Well then I think it's time for you to go to bed.
Give Mommy a kiss.

BILLY: Goodnight, Mommy.

(BILLY *kisses* CLAIRE *and lies down in his crib.* CLAIRE
*picks up the coloring book and looks through it, clearly very
worried.*)

## Scene VI

JANE: Everything will be all right. I will be here, right
here. There's nothing to worry about.

BILLY: Are you sure?

JANE: I promise you, Billy. I will take care of
everything. You'll be okay.

BILLY: I see everybody else. And I see me. I know I'm
not supposed to be three years old.

JANE: So why then?

BILLY: Because Mommy takes care of me.

JANE: There's got to be more to it than that.

BILLY: Mommy needs me. Really needs me. I don't know why. I just know that if I go outside, something really bad will happen to me.

JANE: How do you know that?

BILLY: Because Mommy told me so. He wouldn't lie.

JANE: And you believe everything he says?

BILLY: He's my Mommy.

JANE: What if...just what if, okay? What if what Claire tells you is wrong?

BILLY: It's not!

JANE: I know...but what if? What if she...he...really believes it to be true and right, but it's really wrong?

BILLY: But mommies are never wrong. That's why they're mommies. They know everything.

JANE: But, Billy...

BILLY: That's the reason that mommies are mommies, because they have to take care of their little boys and girls. And they can't be wrong or little boys and girls get torn apart by mean doggies and fall out the window and get hit by big cars and get their heads bashed and their brains leak out all over the sidewalk. And they die.

JANE: Well, let's not dwell on that, okay? We have some very important work to do. You ready?

BILLY: I'm scared.

JANE: I know. It's not easy to look back at the hard times in your life. But many times we have to, in order to make sense out of who we are.

BILLY: I know who I am! I'm Billy!

JANE: And that's a really good start. But Billy has a lot of memories and a lot of feelings and…well, look at it this way: What does Billy want?

BILLY: I told you. I want to do makelove. I wanna do makelove with you!

JANE: Billy. You know that is not part of the bargain. That is something that comes later with someone special. And it will. Do you understand?

BILLY: No.

JANE: Sometimes you have to really, really believe in what you're doing, Billy. Even if you don't get what you want, sometimes you get something you didn't expect. Something better.

BILLY: What if you don't get nothing?

JANE: That's always a possibility. That's what taking a chance means. You can always lose, Billy. That's part of life.

BILLY: But I don't want to lose.

JANE: Nobody ever does. But we do sometimes.

BILLY: That's not fair.

JANE: I know. I don't like it either. Now. What else does Billy want?

BILLY: I…wanna be a big boy. I wanna go outside and play. I wanna…

JANE: Come on, Billy. Tell me what you really, really want.

BILLY: I want Mommy to come home.

JANE: Mommy will be home at five-thirty, like always.

BILLY: No! Not five-thirty Mommy! I want Mommy-Mommy!

JANE: Mommy-Mommy? You mean…

BILLY: I want Mommy-Mommy.

JANE: Right. Wow. Okay, Billy...

BILLY: I don't wanna talk to the camera.

JANE: Maybe if you talk about it—maybe—if you talk about Mommy-Mommy to the camera, and my professor sees it, then maybe we can something learn about Mommy. Mommy-Mommy.

BILLY: No. No more camera!

JANE: Okay, Billy...

BILLY: I want something now.

JANE: Billy, now you said you would. You said you were going to finish the Billy book, remember?

BILLY: I don't care about the stupid Billy book. I spend every day up here. I'm scared of going outside. I'm scared of cars, doggies, policemen. I know I have to go outside, but if I do that, then...

JANE: Then what?

BILLY: I'll be grown up. I won't need Mommy anymore.

JANE: That will be a good thing, Billy.

BILLY: What would happen to Mommy?

JANE: Mommy would have to take care of himself. He's taken care of you all this time. Who goes to work every day?

BILLY: Mommy...

JANE: Who cooks all the meals?

BILLY: Mommy does, but...

JANE: Claire is a big boy, Billy.

BILLY: But Mommy will be all alone. I'll have lots of friends, but Mommy won't. Will *you* take care of Mommy?

JANE: Oh, no, Billy. No. I can't do that, Billy. I can't.

BILLY: You keep wanting me to do things, talk to the camera, go out, tell stories. But you don't give me nothing. *(He grabs video camera, runs to opposite side of stage)* Then No! No more talking! No more camera! You can just go away. Go away and never come back.

JANE: Billy. Billy! Just tell me the story. Tell me the story first…and then we'll see, okay?

*(BILLY turns his back on her)*

BILLY: I spy with my little eye…

JANE: Billy? Billy?

BILLY: How important is it to you to finish this?

*(JANE stares at BILLY. Standoff. She makes a decision and exits the room. BILLY looks after her, then follows offstage, dropping the video camera on the couch)*

## Scene VII

*(JANE exits bedroom wrapped in a sheet, carrying clothes.)*

JANE: William, will you be all right for two minutes? I need to go potty and clean up.

BILLY: Okay.

*(JANE exits to bathroom. BILLY enters living room; he is dressed only in his diaper.)*

BILLY: "William." Big boys get called "William". Big boys…get to go outside! And I can have a bike! And I can…do makelove! I can have a cigarette!

*(BILLY looks at JANE's bag, then opens it, removes a pack of cigarettes and pack of matches, which he stares at fixedly. CLAIRE enters front door as she exits bathroom, still half dressed.)*

JANE: Whoops.

CLAIRE: *Omigod!* What …?

JANE: Oh, shit…Claire…

CLAIRE: Omigod. You…you…filthy little…child molester!

BILLY: Mommy—!

JANE: Child…? Ferchrissakes, Claire, calm down.

CLAIRE: *Whore! (He lunges at* JANE.*)* Slut! *Bitch!*

BILLY: Mommy! Stop!

CLAIRE: And you! You…

JANE: Claire! Stop!

BILLY: Mommy…

CLAIRE: Did you…? With her…?

BILLY: I…

CLAIRE: You did. Omigod. You little…and what are you doing with matches?!!

JANE: Billy! Give me those back!

BILLY: I am a big boy now!

*(*JANE *grabs matches and cigarettes from* BILLY.*)*

CLAIRE: Get those matches out of my house! Get them out! Now!

JANE: Fine. *(She replaces cigarettes and matches in her bag.)*

CLAIRE: No! Get them out! Get them out!

JANE: Ferchrissake, Claire—

CLAIRE: Throw water on them! Throw them in the toilet!

JANE: All right, Claire! *(She throws matches out window.)* Okay! They're gone!

CLAIRE: You leave my house this instant!

JANE: That's what I'm doing. William, get ready to go.

CLAIRE: What? You are not going anywhere! Go to your crib! *Now!*

JANE: William, it's okay. Go get your big boy / clothes on.

CLAIRE: I told you to go to your crib!

BILLY: I don't need a crib anymore! Big boys don't sleep in cribs!

CLAIRE: I am your Mommy and you will listen to me!

BILLY: No. I'm going with babysitter Jane!

JANE: This is his decision, Claire.

CLAIRE: What?!

JANE: That's right, Claire. It will be okay, William. Don't be afraid. I'll look out for you.

CLAIRE: Oh, you will, will you? What makes you think you're qualified to take care of Billy?

JANE: To start with, you've been paying me to do that for over a year already.

CLAIRE: So now you want to do it full-time? You're going to cook his meals? Change his diapers? Read him his bedtime stories?

JANE: No, Claire. All that is over. No more diapers. No more bedtime stories.

BILLY: Babysitter Jane is going to make me famous!

CLAIRE: *(Sotto voce)* Omigod.

BILLY: I'm going to be in a book! A book all about me!

CLAIRE: She's filling your head with lies, Billy.

JANE: No, I'm not, Claire.

CLAIRE: A "book"? Tell him the truth, Jane. Not just the sunny-summer-day fantasy. It's not a book, it's a study. Tell him what will really happen.

BILLY: But Mommy, I wanna go with babysitter Jane. The professors wanna talk to me!

CLAIRE: Is that what you're telling him? That he'll have important professor friends? He'll be important? Well, that's just all shiny peachy dandy.

JANE: Claire…please. I didn't want this it to happen this way, but…you have to let him go, or Billy—William—will be here for the rest of his life.

CLAIRE: Billy has everything he needs right here!

JANE: This is wrong. You know it's wrong. I promise you: William will get the best attention possible…

CLAIRE: Your friends, your professors…will take one look at us and make him into a sideshow.

JANE: That is not true!

CLAIRE: Why do you hate me so much? I've never been anything but kind and welcoming to you.

JANE: Kind and—? You treat me like a doormat!

CLAIRE: I welcome you into my home and entrust you with everything in the world / that I care about—

JANE: And you have nothing to worry about! No harm will come to William. I promise you.

CLAIRE: Billy, please. Don't do this.

BILLY: But I wanna…I wanna grow up, Mommy. I wanna go do things outside…I wanna meet people…

CLAIRE: Billy! Listen to me. She's making it look like you'll be someplace perfect, but it won't be.

JANE: You're hardly qualified to make judgments on what's perfect. Or even healthy.

CLAIRE: And you're qualified to judge how a mother raises her son?

JANE: Mother? Claire, you're his big brother.

CLAIRE: I'm his Mommy.

BILLY: You're just Claire-Mommy. You're not Mommy-Mommy.

CLAIRE: I am the Mommy who's raised you, fed you, clothed you, played with you, and cooked your meals for twenty-seven years!

JANE: Please, Claire. He needs to leave here! Go, Billy. Go get your big boy clothes on.

CLAIRE: Billy, you march straight into Mommy's bedroom and wait for me right there!

BILLY: No! I'm going with babysitter Jane! *(He starts to gather toys and a blanket from crib.)*

CLAIRE: You have no idea what it takes. Who will care for him the way his mommy does? Who, Jane?

JANE: You think *you've* given him the best care? We'll see what the doctors have to say about that.

BILLY: Doctors? *(Drops toys, clutches blanket)*

CLAIRE: Yes, Billy. Doctors!

BILLY: No! No doctors! No doctors!

CLAIRE: Oh…didn't Jane tell you that all her friends would be doctors?

BILLY: No doctors! No! No hospital!

JANE: William, it's okay. They're good doctors! They're—

BILLY: *(Covers head with blanket)*
Hospitals are big and white;
With ambulances and flashing lights;
The doctors' knives go snip and cut;
And rip Billy open and tear out his guts!

JANE: *No!* There's nothing to worry about!

BILLY: You never said nothing about doctors.

JANE: I didn't know you felt this way. You never said anything.

BILLY: Doctors hurt people…

JANE: No, William. They'll just talk. They'll ask you questions. They won't hurt you. I promise.

BILLY: *(Takes blanket from his head)* Will you be with me?

JANE: Right by your side. Every minute. Please trust me.

CLAIRE: Billy, you can't go…you can't leave me…

BILLY: Babysitter Jane will keep me safe. She promised.

CLAIRE: She promises this, she promises that. She promises you everything. And what about me?

JANE: What about you?

CLAIRE: Yes! What happens to me? Where do I go? What do I do when Billy is gone?

JANE: It's not the end of the world, Claire. You'll survive.

CLAIRE: Tell him I'll still be his Mommy. If you can't, Little Miss Promisemaker, then tell him why he'll never see me again.

BILLY: What?

CLAIRE: Billy…her doctor friends will read that thesis of hers and take me away from you.

BILLY: No! They won't!

CLAIRE: Tell him the truth, Jane!

JANE: That's all he's ever gotten from me. Can you say the same thing?

CLAIRE: You'll never see me again, Billy. The doctors won't allow it. Will they, Jane? And I won't be your Mommy anymore.

BILLY: No! No!

JANE: Oh my God, Claire, look at what you're doing to him! Don't you love him at all?

CLAIRE: Love him? I love him / more than you ever could.

JANE: / —Claire, you have to listen to me—

CLAIRE: Do *you* love him, Jane? Tell him you love him.

JANE: William…listen to me. I know what's best for you. You have to trust me. If you don't trust me, you'll be here forever. No going out. No bike. No making decisions like a big boy. No more chances to do makelove. You know what your life will be like. William? Look at me. William!

CLAIRE: Do you love him?

JANE: You have to leave home. You have to start taking care of yourself.

CLAIRE: Now he's on his own? What happened to all the wonderful people who would take care of him?

JANE: William, this is part of growing up. That's what being a big boy is.

CLAIRE: Living alone.

JANE: You'll have your very own apartment!

CLAIRE: No one to cook your meals.

JANE: You can eat whatever you want. Whenever you want to.

CLAIRE: No one to do your laundry.

JANE: Big boys do their own laundry.

CLAIRE: Tell him you'll love him the way his Mommy does. Billy, listen to her. Say it, Jane.

JANE: William, you know you have to do this. I know it's scary. I know it is.

CLAIRE: Listen to her, Billy. She can't say it.

JANE: Trust me, William. You'll never be a big boy if you stay home!

BILLY: I don't know…

CLAIRE: Billy—

BILLY: *Mommy be quiet!* *(To* JANE*)* I love you. I wanna marry you.

CLAIRE: Do you see what you're doing to him?

JANE: William…I know you have feelings, but…

BILLY: I love you.

JANE: And I told you…I told you…oh god…wait…

CLAIRE: Understand, Billy? Do you understand? You leave here, and no one will ever love you the way I do.

JANE: *Claire!*

CLAIRE: No one who will love you the way I do. No one, Billy. You'll have to find someone to love you, and it won't be easy. Jane doesn't. Jane doesn't love you at all.

JANE: That's not true!

CLAIRE: Then tell him that! *(Beat)* You aren't much, are you?

JANE: *(To* CLAIRE *alone)* This is all your fault, isn't it? Were you playing with matches, Claire? Is that what happened?

CLAIRE: Tell him how much you love him.

JANE: You're sick, Claire. You're a fucking psycho.

CLAIRE: I'm his Mommy.

JANE: Oh god. William, please listen to me. If you don't come with me, then everything we've done, all the stories we've told, all the video, the whole Billy project…it won't be worth anything. It won't happen.

CLAIRE: Especially when they find out you slept with your thesis subject.

JANE: William…please…all my research…everything I have…is about you. I need you, William. I need you…

BILLY: I love you.

JANE: William, I…

*(Beat)*

BILLY: My name is Billy.

JANE: No…William. It's William. You're a big boy. William…

CLAIRE: I think you just lost. Missy.

JANE: You know he needs to leave here. You know it!

CLAIRE: He'll do just fine here with me. He always has. My baby boy needs extra care because he is soooo…

BILLY: *(Barely audible)* Special.

JANE: But Claire…

BILLY: Mommy loves me all the time
He cooks my meals and tells me rhymes
He keeps me safe in my little world
Mommy is my bestest girl.
I'm sorry…

JANE: Oh, Billy…

CLAIRE: Leave. Now.

(JANE *looks at* BILLY, *then turns and walks out the door.* CLAIRE *crosses to front door, locks it.*)

CLAIRE: It's okay, Billy. Shh. It's okay. She's gone now. She's gone away…and she'll never come back.

BILLY: But I wanted to grow up. I wanted…

CLAIRE: You will, Billy. One of these days. You'll be a big boy before you know it. Trust Mommy.

BILLY: I want Mommy-Mommy!

CLAIRE: Listen to me, Billy.

(BILLY *starts to cross to* CLAIRE.)

No. Sit there. Now listen to me. Are you listening?

BILLY: Yes...

CLAIRE: Good boy. Now. You can't have Mommy-Mommy. She won't be coming back. Ever. All you'll ever have is me, Billy. I am your only Mommy. I'm all you'll ever need. And I love you so much. Do you love Mommy?

BILLY: *(Pause)* Yes...

(CLAIRE *crosses to stool.)*

CLAIRE: That's good, Billy. You should love only Mommy. Now come here and let Mommy hold you.

(BILLY *sits between* CLAIRE's *legs, arms around his waist and hugs.)*

CLAIRE: Oh, yes. That's my baby. Yes, Billy. Hold me tight. Mommy will take care of you. Mommy will get you everything you need. Because Mommy loves you more than anybody. You're Mommy's baby. Mommy's world. Let Mommy hold you tight and protect—

(BILLY *reaches over to* CLAIRE's *breast.)*

CLAIRE: Billy? What are you—

(BILLY *rips* CLAIRE's *shirt open.)*

Omigod. Billy! No! You shouldn't...You...

(BILLY *tries to breastfeed.)*

CLAIRE: Okay, Billy. Yes. Mommy has you now. Mommy will take care of you. Mommy will always take care of you. That's right. That's good. Yes, Billy. Yes. Yes.

Mockingbird, little Mockingbird

Gonna buy my baby boy a mockingbird
And if that mockingbird tries to fly
Gonna sit on him and make him cry
If he don't cry and tries to sing
Gonna tie him up in my apron string
And if that apron string don't hold
He's gonna surely break my heart of gold

END OF PLAY

www.ingramcontent.com/pod-product-compliance
Lightning Source LLC
Chambersburg PA
CBHW070031110426
42741CB00035B/2729